God's Rarest Diamonds:

A Proverbs Life after Divorce Devotional for Women

By Charis Rooks

Edited by: Claude R. Royston

BK Royston Publishing, LLC
Jeffersonville, IN

BK Royston Publishing
P. O. Box 4321
Jeffersonville, IN 47131
502-802-5385
http://bkroystonpublishing.com
bkroystonpublishing@gmail.com

Published by: BK Royston Publishing LLC
Cover photo licensed by: Shutterstock.com
Layout: BK Royston Publishing LLC
Scripture listings: King James Version

ISBN-13: 978-0692498040

ISBN-10: 0692498044

LCCN: 2015947699

Printed in the United States of America

Thank You

To my Heavenly Father I thank you for your son Jesus Christ. I thank you for being there when no one else was there. I thank you for waking me up each and every day loving and encouraging me. I thank you father God for giving me the passion to work with women in the area of divorce recovery. I thank you Father for allowing my recovery from two divorces and for turning my past hurt into my purpose and healing. Father, thank you again for your son, my personal lord and savior Jesus Christ.

Jesus I thank you because you are my surgeon (healer) who mended my heart again after not one but two divorces. I thank you Jesus for being my therapist who took the time to not only develop but also implement my rehabilitation after not one but two divorces. Jesus no matter what when I call your name you are there I never have to look for you or ask has anyone seen you. You are there regardless of the situation and I thank you for that. It was a many of days I know you had to carry me because I just couldn't walk anymore. When I hit my lowest Jesus, it was only you who I heard when I felt my life was no longer significant. Thank you Jesus for loving me when I felt alone, guiding me when I felt lost, and carrying me when I was broken from my divorce.

To my daughters Briana and Katelyn

I thank you both for being great young women of God. You both are such a blessing whom God has entrusted to me to disciple. You both have ministered to me in many ways that I can't begin to explain. I thank God every day that he has allowed me to raise two of HIS rarest precious diamonds. No, it hasn't been easy for us but God has blessed me with the both of you who no matter what have shown me love unconditionally. Not many can say their children speak His Word over their life. Two daughters who pray for me, lay hands on me when I'm sick, and who look at me and tell me that not only do they love me but God loves me too and God loved me first. It's those moments that I see how God loved me so much he gave me two of his most treasured gifts. Thank you BB and KK

To my mother Kem

Mom, I am so blessed in life to have you as my mother. I must say I have looked up to you all my life. You have been there for me no matter what. Through all my successes and failures you were right there either loving me when I needed to be loved or fussing at me when I needed to get fussed at, and praying for me when I needed prayer. Your constant unwavering faith in God and our Lord and Savior Jesus Christ is my motivation. I have seen over the years what you have had to endure and how you called on the name of Jesus every single time. I watched how even though everything was never perfect or what you may have wanted, it always worked out for HIS good. Mom I can always look next to me and see you. You tell me when I'm correct or incorrect and you let me make the decision. You have held my hand from my childhood to my adulthood and you still refuse to let my hand go. Let's just say there were a few times I wouldn't have blamed you for letting go however, you didn't. Mom I just want to say thank you I ask God daily to bless you with His favor. You always have been and always will be my lady bug. I love you ma.

To my brothers Martellus and Marcel

You both have created a sibling bond with me that I'm so blessed to have and never will let go. We fuss, we fight, we have our hissy fits but at the end of the day we regroup and make up. I love that you both are so supportive of me and my dreams. Never have you said you don't see me achieving and never have you said you won't be there for me. You are my personal hustlers making sure your sister gets her message out through her writing. I would not trade either of you for the world.

To Kent

Last but certainly not least. They say you save the best for last so here we go. We have been through it haven't we Kent? We started off as best friends, lovers, parents, married, divorced, co-parent, and now best friends again. It seems like we have come full circle in our relationship if you ask me. You have shown me how much God loves me to restore our relationship in order for me to move forward and help other women on their journey of healing. I thank you for being there for no matter what. It was your constant prayer for me and our girls that helped guide me to healing our family in our brokenness. Your trust and faith in God has inspired me to progress in my trust in faith that God has something awesome in store for me, you and our girls. To the young man whom I met in college who wanted to pour me some Gatorade, I could never imagine that in that moment you would over a period of time pour Love into me the way that you always have. As we always have said since the very first time we said it "Love you for life" Kent.

Introduction

It is not unusual if you do not feel on top of the world when all the divorce processes are over. When you finally get a chance to sit alone in the quiet, no matter the reason for your divorce, for some those moments tend to be overwhelming. These moments in time feel as if you are a new student at college or a new employee on the job who missed orientation. You have no idea what will happen and actually no idea of where you should go, however you must deal with it. You signed on to a work contract or your tuition has been paid in full. In other words what you do know in this moment in time is there is no turning back. The divorce is now final. So you ask yourself, "Where will I go from here?" Allow the next 90 days of empowerment devotions to help you navigate through this sense of being a foreigner in your own life. Allow these words of encouragement to be the notes that the professor or supervisor hands to you on the first day of work/classes to catch you up on what you missed at orientation. Use these to help you as you fill in the gaps of your personal journey of life after divorce. As you read your daily devotional really study the book of Proverbs and its amazing life changing guidance that God has blessed us with. I highly recommend that you read one a day and really focus on and study areas of your life that you may need to open the door of wisdom for. I encourage you to journal along with me as we travel along this this journey called life after divorce together.

Day 1

Do not be tempted to feel sorry for yourself; you are strong no matter what anyone says. It is always hard to believe that a divorce can happen without fault being assigned to one party or the other; though it may seem like it is your fault, you should not feel sorry for yourself but rather draw strength from your experience and set out with healing and personal growth in mind. During these first few days following a divorce you should take the time to set smaller goals for yourself. Though it may be tempting to set huge goals in order to feel the sense of accomplishment that they bring, it is much more satisfying to set smaller goals that are readily attainable so that you are less likely to experience disappointment. Small goals can also help you get through the day and really get toward healing. Know your own self-worth and strength.

She is clothed with strength and dignity, and she laughs without fear of the future.   Proverbs 31:25

Day 2

Don't sweat the small stuff. If you are overwhelmed sit down and take a minute to breathe. Though it may be tempting to do everything that you normally do and pretend that nothing is wrong, this is not going to help you in the long run. Instead, focus on one thing at a time and if the dishes do not get done or the wash is a day late, do not fall apart. Instead, focus on what you can do and what you are able to get completed, this will make you feel ten times better and will help you focus on your own personal path to God and path to your own recovery. Eventually doing things like the laundry and getting everything done on a normal schedule will be an everyday thing, but immediately following divorce it is far better to take it one day and one task at a time.

Above all else, guard your heart, for everything you do flows from it. Proverbs 4:23

Day 3

Do not be tempted to sin or retaliate. Often times when we are hurt the first thing we want to do is to inflict the same hurt on others. In many cases, it may seem like the only way to feel good about yourself is to make others feel equally bad. Though this may seem like a viable option, you should be the bigger person and focus instead on what you can do to make yourself feel better. It is always best to focus any negative energy that you have on things that are positive and that can help you toward recovery. Instead of dwelling on what has happened or spending time thinking of ways you can make the other party unhappy, focus each day on one thing that you can do to lift your own spirits and build your own confidence and build toward growing and recovering in a safe and healthy manner.

My son, if sinners entice you, do not give in to them. Proverbs 1:10

Day 4

In the beginning shortly after the tears and the
sleepless nights you may encounter a hot temper.
Some days you may not even want to have a bad
temper but it will seem more natural for you to
have a hot temper then to have a cool one.   This
isn't effective healing for yourself nor is it
guarding your heart from more pain. Start a goal
and operate in the mentality that peace is more
important to you than war. When you start to
embrace peace you will notice things that weren't
in your favor will now change to be in your favor.
You will be blessed when your temper is under
control and stays calm.

A hot-tempered person starts fights; a cool-
tempered person stops them. Proverb 15:18

Day 5

Some normalcy can help. Though it may seem like normalcy is never going to be a part of your life again, it may help to do mundane tasks to take your mind off the bigger picture. If you are feeling like you have too much on your shoulders, take a breather and read a book, take a walk outside to clear your mind, do something that you would normally do that helps calm you. Though things are changing you can have a brilliant new life full of love and caring and devotion not only to God and the Gospel but also to those people who love you and who have stuck by your side through it all. Take a moment, relax, and do something that is normal enough that you can forget your troubles long enough to regain your composure so you can recover and tackle your own issues.

The name of the LORD is a strong tower; the righteous run to it and are safe. Proverbs 18:10

Day 6

It's ok to listen to positive advice from others, it may help and you may not use it at all. Though advice right now is probably the last thing you want to listen to, there are plenty of people who are worth listening to. It is always helpful to hear from others who have been through similar trials. If you have a friend or colleague who has dealt with divorce it may be beneficial for you to ask questions about how they dealt with it, how they began to recover, and what tips they may have for your own recovery.

If you had responded to my rebuke, I would have poured out my heart to you and made my thoughts known to you. Proverbs 1:23

Day 7

Do not be afraid to draw strength from your favorite Bible passages. If you have a favorite passage that you draw strength from do not be afraid to let others know where you are getting courage. If you feel the need to take your Bible with you or to take your favorite passage written on a scrap of paper, go ahead and do it. Do not feel ashamed that you need someone to lean on, that you need God and his word to help you through the day. If it makes you feel better go ahead and do it and it will help you in the long run to feel comfortable in your recovery.

For the LORD gives wisdom, and from his mouth come knowledge and understanding. Proverbs 2:6

Day 8

Positivity from friends and family is more helpful than trashing your ex-spouse. If your family or friends want to trash the person you are divorcing, that type of negativity is far more harmful than it is helpful. Though it may seem like this is the best option, it will only bring more negativity into your life and make it even tougher for you to begin your own recovery. Though it may seem impossible to let the past live in the past, it is far better for your personal healing to let go and focus on yourself more than you focus on your ex. Personal healing often begins with letting go and letting go of any animosity is the first step to being able to focus on yourself and focus on your own healing exclusively.

Thus you will walk in the ways of good men and keep to the paths of the righteous. Proverbs 2:20

Day 9

Remember those who stood by you when things got tough. It is always good to feel like you are wanted and often when someone stands by your side they will continue to through thick and thin. Now is the time to let those people know that they are helping you, that they are doing what they can, and that they are making your life better for being in it. If you have a special friend who has done for you while you dealt with this difficult time, take a moment to thank them, to tell them how grateful you are for their help, and let them know that you appreciate them and everything they do and that you want them by your side for the rest of your journey.

Let love and faithfulness never leave you; bind them around your neck, write them on the tablet of your heart. Proverbs 3:3

Day 10

Take time to know that you may not understand, but God does and he has a plan for you. It may seem like everything is topsy turvy and that nothing is in your control. It is difficult for most people to let go and to really let God take the wheel but this is a time when it is more important than anything else. If you have a chance, really let go and let God, do it. The feeling of release and peace of mind when you let go and you really stop worrying is far more fulfilling than any other feeling. God has a plan for you, though you may not agree with every bump that you encounter or every hill you have to climb, they were placed there to help make you a better, stronger person and you should embrace them and let them help you grow and progress toward recovery.

Trust in the LORD with all your heart and lean not on your own understanding; 6 in all your ways acknowledge him, and he will make your paths straight. Proverbs 3: 5-6

Day 11

Your path may not be clear but you can make it.
Some days are going to be far harder than others.
At times it may seem like you are not going the
right way that you are not making the progress that
you feel you should be. These are the days when
you should lean heavily on God and on the fact
that you have a path, it just may not be crystal
clear at that exact moment. Let yourself go, let the
path be a bit foggy and go forth with the
understanding that God loves you and is at your
side.

Have no fear of sudden disaster or of the ruin that
overtakes the wicked, 26 for the LORD will be
your confidence and will keep your foot from
being snared. Proverbs 3: 25-26

Day 12

Take each day as it comes, try not to plan too far ahead. Though it may be tempting to plan out each and every day from here on out so that nothing surprises you or hurts you again, it is far better to take small steps and set one foot in front of the other. Take a few days to just do what comes naturally then start to plan a day ahead, a few days ahead, working up to making longer term plans so that you can better regain your sense of self and create a new sense of normalcy.

Commit to the LORD whatever you do, and he will establish your plans. Proverbs 16:3

Day 13

Let yourself laugh. Laughter is often the best medicine. Though it may seem that you should be dour and unhappy, do not deny yourself happiness and laughter no matter what others think. If you feel like laughing, go right ahead. If others frown, forget what they say and just let yourself be happy. There is no real way to start healing if you do not do so with an optimistic heart and the best way to boost your optimism is to realize that there are still wonderful things in the world and you deserve to be happy.

A cheerful heart is good medicine, but a crushed spirit dries up the bones. Proverbs 17:22

Day 14

Learn, take the time to better yourself, this will help you not only feel better but also begin to heal. Knowledge is said to be one of the greatest weapons that anyone can possess and this is true for those who are struggling with divorce in many ways. It may not seem like a fun or carefree thing to do, but you just endured a legal proceeding that impacted your life. Having knowledge can help you strive to better your own understanding of what is going on. In fact you can really be empowered to realize that you are far stronger than you ever imagined. You do have it in you to be something more and to really be the strong woman that everyone knows you are.

Wisdom is supreme; therefore get wisdom.
Though it cost all you have, get understanding.
Proverbs 4:7

Day 15

Do not speak ill of those who have wronged you, that sort of negativity will do you no good. Again, though it may make you feel better for a moment or two to talk down about your ex or to talk about their new partner, it will not help you on your own positive journey. It is far more productive to focus on your own strengths and on your own good traits and how you are going to use them to not only rebuild your life but also to become the person you want to be after a divorce.

Put away perversity from your mouth; keep corrupt talk far from your lips. Proverbs 4:24

Day 16

Let those that love you help, it does not make you weaker, it only makes you stronger. If you have a sister, a mother, a brother, a friend, let them help you. If your loved ones want to help you with housework, want to help you talk through things, or they just want to be near you, let them. It will ultimately help you to become a stronger person and will help you to become the woman you want to be, a woman who does not depend on pettiness or on anyone else but a woman who allows others to help her therefore, showing true strength.

As iron sharpens iron, so one person sharpens another. Proverbs 27:17

Day 17

Let the Lord into your heart as you start your new journey. Though it may seem as if you are the only one making decisions, the Lord does work in mysterious ways as they say and he is putting decisions before you to see how you handle them. If you let the Lord into your heart you can begin to see where he is guiding you. Ultimately, God only puts the options in front of you, how you handle them is your own decision and your own path. Though the Lord does have his hand in your own personal journey, you must take the first step if you ever want to get to the final destination that he has planned for you.

In their hearts human beings plan their course, but the LORD establishes their steps. Proverbs 16:9

Day 18

Admit that you need help, admit that you are broken and that you are trying to heal and change for the better. This again goes back to the fact that you are in need of help. Though it may seem like you are alone and that you have no real way of healing, you have to admit that you need healing and admit that you need help in order for it to truly help and begin to work. It is one thing to say that you need help but to really start the healing process you must mean it and you have to start working toward that healing in order to truly begin again. Let down any preconceptions that you may have and start to heal in order to really let loose of what is bothering you and work your way toward being a new woman.

Pride goes before destruction, a haughty spirit before a fall. Proverbs 16:18

Day 19

Lean on positivity and make sure you are positive as much as possible. It may seem easy to snap at those who are around you but often a gentle word will help you and those who are also struggling with you. Divorce does not only affect the parents, it affects children, family members, and friends. Therefore, having kind words for yourself and for others can help everyone start to heal. It is far easier to heal if you have a calm and gentle environment and making sure that you use kind words is one way to make sure that everyone is on the same page and everyone is focused on true spiritual and physical healing.

A gentle answer turns away wrath, but a harsh word stirs up anger. Proverbs 15:1

Day 20

It is not easy understanding and dealing with children lashing out. If you do not have children that are involved in your divorce this may not apply so much to your own situation. This can be interpreted in several different ways but the most useful perhaps is to understand that a child has no concept of why mommy and daddy are fighting; they do not understand why one parent is not living with them anymore. This may result in behavior problems and while it may seem like the right thing to do to smother them with affection and allow them to get away with nasty or unpleasant behavior, it is far better to explain to them as best you can and continue to set boundaries that if broken, will come with punishment. A firm hand will give children guidance in this time of need but it can still afford them love.

Those who spare the rod hate their children, but those who love them are careful to discipline them. Proverbs 13:24

Day 21

Let others know how your personal healing is progressing. In most cases, they will share in your victories which will make them that much more meaningful and will make the journey easier. A support group is a great way to make sure you have people that know your struggle and who want to see you succeed. There are plenty of programs out there that have teachers and leaders who can give you advice and who will cheer you on when you succeed.

A friend loves at all times, and a brother is born for a time of adversity. Proverbs 17:17

Day 22

Stick with what you have decided. Though it may seem easy to waiver in what you have set your mind to, do not let others take your mind off of your goals and do not let them sway you in your determination. Determination and steely resolve is the backbone of any recovery plan and once you have chosen the path to your own recovery, don't waiver unless you feel comfortable doing so or unless it is your idea to do so.

The highway of the upright avoids evil; those who guard their ways preserve their lives.
Proverbs 16:17

Day 23

Struggle through not knowing and strive for personal understanding. Though it may be painful to confront your own demons that is the only way you can get past them. Take this time to really think about what is bothering you, about what is breaking your spirit, and resolve to change it, resolve to let it go and let yourself truly be free of it. Try to understand yourself because true understanding is the only thing that is going to help you recover.

The beginning of wisdom is this: Get wisdom. Though it cost you all you have, get understanding. Proverbs 4:7

Day 24

Keep the gospel close; you never know when you will need an extra bit of encouragement, when you may need that little boost to keep you going. Keep your Bible near and keep your favorite passages on hand and actually read them from time to time. It may even help to read your Bible daily to draw inspiration from the stories of those that have suffered and overcome with the help of the Lord.

Get wisdom, get understanding; do not forget my words or turn away from them. Proverbs 4:5

Day 25

Do not let other people charm you or convince you to do things you do not feel comfortable with. If you feel like it is a bad idea or that you do not want to do it, do not be pushed for the sake of your friends or people whom you know. Make sure you stay strong and true to the person you are and want to be.

Charm is deceptive, and beauty is fleeting; but a woman who fears the LORD is to be praised.
Proverbs 31:30

Day 26

Let go and just relax, it is hard enough being a mother, a friend, and so much more. You should take a day or so every so often to really relax and let yourself rest. If you want to sit on the couch one day and watch movies, if it will help your personal healing, do it, just go for it. Sometimes our brains need to really just shut down for a little while and rest and during a time as stressful as going through a divorce, sometimes rest can do wonders.

In all your ways submit to him, and he will make your paths straight. Proverbs 3:6

Day 27

God put you here for a reason, he created you, he molded you, and he has loved you, do not ever forget that. Though it may seem that you are getting an unfair rap, it is happening for a reason. God does not make mistakes and it is more important now than ever to realize this.

The LORD brought me forth as the first of his works, before his deeds of old; Proverbs 8:22

Day 28

Simplify. This may seem that it is coming a little late in the game but simplifying can do so much for you. Take away all the excess baggage and just focus on today. Simplify and see how much you can achieve. Focus on yourself, on your family, and on your friends and you will be amazed at how much more satisfying life can be and how much easier it is to just live.

Go to the ant, you sluggard; consider its ways and be wise! Proverbs 6:6

Day 29

Understanding will come to you through God with time. It is not an immediate fix but God will help you if you call out for help and you continue to keep him in your heart even after you feel you have been healed. It may seem like you have used him for healing and you can stop worrying so much, but God can continue to help you grow long after the wounds of divorce have scabbed over.

Indeed, if you call out for insight and cry aloud for understanding. Proverbs 2:3

Day 30

Up until this point you have been dragged through the mud, put through the wringer, and you feel that you have finally started to heal. At this point you just need to love yourself. Know that God loves you, that your family loves you, that your friends love you and that you have purpose, potential, and value. You are here for a reason, you are loved, and you have been put through all the trials that you have dealt with because you are meant to be so much more.

Many are the plans in a human heart, but it is the LORD's purpose that prevails. Proverbs 19:21

Testimony

So you may be asking yourself right now how in the world can I give when I'm struggling myself? What can I offer I'm divorced? I remember a young woman shortly after my divorce asking me did I have any advice for her. She was engaged and overheard that I had recently divorced. She didn't want to go into her marriage without some advice to protect her and her future husband from divorce. Well, she happened to ask me on what I would say was one of my "low days". My response to her question was "girl whatever you do don't do it. You do not want to end up like me". Yes I did give freely but I gave freely a negative advice that stemmed from my hurt and pain. I was giving but also being stingy at the same time. I say stingy because God will place you in strategic places so that complete strangers may cross your path and you are positioned at that moment to give freely and not to just divorced women. Yes God will do this right before the divorce, during, and after. Do not make the mistake I made that day instead, testify freely to whatever God has done to prepare you during every stage you are either currently in or have encountered in your past. Share what God has taught you, and how God brought you through your storm. We all have something to give each other and that would be our testimony. Yes, I was divorced but I had the opportunity to help other women through sharing my testimony. My testimony could have very well kept her from going down the same path by only spending a few moments of time with her, and time would have cost me nothing. She was strategically placed in my life so I could give freely to help her but I didn't take advantage of the opportunity that God had given me. I should have said "congratulations on your engagement and I would love to help you." First, I should have asked, "Do both you and your fiancé have a relationship with Christ? Have you taken premarital counseling?" Or I could have said even something as simple as "well let me share my story with you." My questions and testimony then could have helped this young woman embrace her engagement and be strong as she enters into a marriage instead of instilling fear into her.

Your personal testimony is more valuable than many of your possessions. You can change the way that you see yourself, the way that others see you, and the way that you grow and change. Your testimony can help to make you a stronger person while empowering others to make a change in their own lives for the better.

Give freely and become wealthier; be stingy and lose everything. Proverbs 11:24

Day 1

Helping your neighbor could come in the form of something that you could easily give such as listening, encouragement, and prayer. God will give you opportunities in your life to bless others and you are already equipped with everything you need to bless them already. A kind word, a kind look, or something equally small may be all that you need to help someone who needs your help.

If you can help your neighbor now, don't say, Come back tomorrow, and then I'll help you.
Proverbs 3:28

Day 2

You are not only sharing testimony you are sharing truth. When you share truth you are sharing Gods love and in sharing Gods love there is nothing that can top that love absolutely nothing. Therefore, you are a representative of his Kingdom and in doing so you will be attracting people just by your presence. You are to be a beacon of hope to those women who are hearing your testimony, do not squander your time in the spotlight.

The way of the fool is right in his own eyes, but a wise man is he who listens to counsel.
Proverbs 12:15

Day 3

It's ok to let a person know in a gentle loving way, when applicable, that their actions may not have been the best actions to take. So approach this by speaking gentle words of direction through discernment. Sugar coating is not beneficial; it can only hurt in the long run so make sure you are gentle but truthful. You can build others up while giving them constructive criticism if you take the time to think about what you are saying and really think about how you are saying it.

Gentle words are a tree of life; a deceitful tongue crushes the spirit. Proverbs 15:4

Day 4

Your testimony is so very powerful in a sense that there are people who need to hear it and that means all of it. When you alter your testimony you damage the blessing that it is capable of bringing another person. Now I'm not saying your testimony will stop someone from going down the same path as you. What I am saying is offer insight through testimony of truth not testimony of convenience. Everyone has free will and of course everyone's outcome will be different however let's be effective in our testimony and speak truth not half or part but 100% truth no matter how bad your part may be.

A truthful witness saves lives, but a false witness.
Proverbs 14:25

Day 5

When you decide to share your testimony in the
beginning you may have a sense of uneasiness.
This is ok and you should embrace it. The beauty
of sharing is the fact that you will not know who it
will benefit or impact directly or indirectly. You
could speak to 5 people sharing your testimony
and they can pass your story along at work the next
day and it can reach a person who you have never
met. This is the ripple effect of your testimony.
Embrace it and do not shy away from it.

The name of the Lord is a strong tower; the
righteous runs into it and is safe. Proverbs 18:10

Day 6

How do you share your testimony effectively? By answering the following questions when sharing. Where has God brought me from? What has God brought me through? Where has God positioned me now? These questions are guides to effectively share your testimony to others with a purpose of showing the complete picture that God has painted of your life.

He who neglects discipline despises himself, but he who listens to reproof acquires understanding.
Proverbs 15:32

Day 7

Confidence seems to be the area that we suffer the most when making the decision to step out and help others. Many times we sit and we fear or worry about situations that haven't even presented themselves. If you find your self-rehearsing in your head the possible negative responses to your actions remember this, God loves you and he favors no one of his children more than another. What was done for you can be done for others? If you never received deliverance where would you be today? Confidence can make a huge difference and showing others that you are confident can boost their confidence as well.

Watch over your heart with all diligence, for from it flows the springs of life. Proverbs 4:23

Day 8

When it feels like nothing is getting through, nothing is working out right, keep up the good work that you have started. Make sure that you set your sights on success and that you keep fighting for what you think is right. Even if others tell you that you are not making a difference, change does not happen in one day, it takes time to break through. It may not feel like your testimony is doing much for you or for those who listen but it is and that is the truth.

To do righteousness and justice is desired by the Lord more than sacrifice. Proverbs 21:3

Day 9

Make sure that you keep your sights on what really matters. As you share your testimony with others, as you tell your story, remember that you have God in your corner and God is rooting for your success and for the success of those whom you are helping. God is always with you and even when it may seem like you are not making a difference or you are not sure if what you are doing is right, you are making a difference.

Trust in the Lord with all your heart and lean not on your own understanding. Proverbs 3:5

Day 10

The start of real change for your own healing
through testimony and for those that whom you are
telling is to build a strong foundation. If that means
breaking down and showing people the bare bones
and the frame upon which you started to build
yourself up, then do it. If you share your testimony
with others in a way that you feel would bless
them, they will be more likely to be receptive of
your testimony when it comes to helping them.

Start children off on the way they should go, and
even when they are old they will not turn from it.
Proverbs 22:6

Day 11

Though you are helping others with your own testimony, you too can learn from what they have to tell you. Learning through testimony truly is a two way street and you may be able to take as much away from the testimony of those whom you are speaking as they take from you. It may seem like a difficult thing to do, but if you let them tell you their story, you may start to heal in ways that you never expected. You can receive instruction from the women with whom you are working and their own struggle can help you to change and grow as well.

For receiving instruction in prudent behavior, doing what is right and just and fair. Proverbs 1:3

Day 12

Take the time to tell others about your story and do not judge them. Though you may have handled a situation differently than others, it is always important to keep love in your heart. God has love for everyone and his love is everlasting and ever important. His love never leaves you and you should never allow the love you have for others to leave you. Love is stronger than hate, it is stronger than anger. By showing those that you are mentoring love you are giving them the hope that is needed to do so much more than they ever thought possible.

Let love and faithfulness never leave you; bind them around your neck, write them on the tablet of your heart. Proverbs 3:3

Day 13

You should work to give those with whom you are working with understanding and wisdom. They may not be in the same stage of healing as you, they may not even be divorced yet, however, you should give them the understanding that they need to rise above their circumstances. Understanding is so valuable, so important and you are the one who can give the understanding that these women need. You can give them the information, the knowledge that you have acquired and you can truly make a difference with them.

How much better to get wisdom than gold, to choose understanding rather than silver.
Proverbs 16:16

Day 14

Kindness can do so much; kindness can make harsh criticism, harsh advice, and harsh words melt away. You catch more flies with honey than with vinegar and you have the opportunity to show women who may feel like they are not loved, that may feel like they need a kind word realize that God always loves them and that they can grow and get past what they are dealing with. Sometimes a kind word is all that you need to get through a very tough day.

Pleasant words are like a honeycomb, sweetness to the soul and health to the body. Proverbs 16:24

Day 15

Create in the women with whom you speak to a
longing for Christ, a longing for healing, a longing
for self-worth and they will be able to grow and
become stronger on their own. Though it may
seem easy to create a longing, you have to make
sure that they have a longing for success which
will make the journey easier. Hope is a great
motivator and it can also help to create the longing
for Christ that is needed to ultimately succeed and
change the life that you have before you.

Hope deferred makes the heart sick, but a longing
fulfilled is the tree of life. Proverbs 13:12

Day 16

Help women in need find Christ through your own testimony. This is the time when you can tell them stories from your lowest low, your furthest point from success and feeling whole, then tell them how Christ brought you out of your wallowing to become the woman that you are today. You have a chance to show them that Christ is love and through Christ they can heal.

For whoever finds me finds life and receives favor from the Lord. Proverbs 8:35

Day 17

Women are very strong individuals. At times as women, we underestimate our own strengths. Women have the strength to carry a child for nine months, to give birth, to keep a family afloat, and many women do not even know their true worth. This is your chance to show them how strong they truly are.

She sets about her work vigorously; her arms are strong for her tasks. Proverbs 31:17

Day 18

When you are wondering how or what to say regarding sharing your testimony to others remember this. Your testimony is just that, YOUR TESTIMONY. No one can tell your story the way that you can. So know that the delivery of your testimony has no uniform guide. You are the expert and only the expert can explain and deliver the content effectively. Even if you start to feel that you must follow a particular guideline to where someone has you distorting your testimony, please stay away from this type of guidance. Your testimony should not change for anyone because if it does it is no longer your testimony. A great deal of the healing that comes with testimony is being able to tell it your own way without having to worry about what others will think.

The fear of man brings a snare, but he who trusts in the Lord will be exalted. Proverbs 29:25

Day 19

This is a time when you should be building others up but it is also a time for advising others about dangers that they may face. It is important that you help other women learn what temptations may face them, what troubles they may have to deal with, and just what they should be wary of as they take their personal journey toward becoming healed. Caution can be a tremendous tool.

The prudent see danger and take refuge but the simple keep going and suffer for it. Proverbs 27:12

Day 20

Some women may feel the need to talk bad about their ex, to say things they may regret later, to do things that are not going to help them heal. Most people learn by example, this is a time when you can show others that you can still talk kindly about the people that are not part of your life anymore and that this can help them heal. This is your chance to tell those with whom you are sharing your testimony with that it is not going to be easy but that you should not use harsh words to build yourself up because it is not going to help you in the end.

A soft answer turns away wrath, but a harsh word stirs up anger. Proverbs 15:1

Day 21

Now is a time when you can tell the women you are working with that they may have had plans when they were married and they may have had plans that were unfulfilled. This does not make anyone a failure. A woman can make plans for every day of the rest of her life and if her plans are not part of God's plan, they will not come to fruition. It is not wrong or weak to have to abandon plans because your life changed and you are proof of that. Use your testimony to let others see that plans change, but that is not a bad thing.

Many are the plans in man's heart, but it is the Lords purpose that prevails. Proverbs 19:21

Day 22

Let others know that you are happy with the life that you have chosen. Your testimony is a chance to tell others that you may not have everything that you had before the divorce, but you have everything you need with your own strength and with what God has provided. He knows what you need, he knows what you have and he knows how to give you just what you need to succeed and rise above the challenges that you have before you.

Two things I ask of you, O Lord; do not refuse me before I die. Keep falsehood and lies far from me; give me neither poverty nor riches, but give me only my daily bread. Otherwise, I may have too much and disown you and say, "Who is the Lord?" Or I may become poor and steal, and so dishonor the name of my God. Proverbs 30:7-9

Day 23

Testimony is a fantastic way to show others the discipline and structure that can be obtained even when your life is upside down. Sometimes having structure is all that you need to make your day seem a little less awful. Structure and discipline can help make sense of a topsy turvy world and your personal testimony may be just what it takes to help these women to make a routine, to make rules, to make structure that can help them get on the path to healing.

Mark a life of discipline and live wisely; do not squander your precious life. Proverbs 8:33

Day 24

There is an amazing strength in numbers. This is a chance for your testimony to show others that you could not do it alone but with Christ and your own support group you were able to achieve happiness, you were able to heal. Christ is the ultimate advisor and with his help you can do anything and you can rise above your own personal turmoil to become something more. With Christ you can do anything and with Christ you can make a true change in your own life and in the lives of those around you. With Christ you can truly use your testimony to change lives.

Plans fail for lack of counsel, but with many advisors they succeed. Proverbs 15:22

Day 25

Your testimony can help show others their intense strength. Most women do not know what they are truly capable of until they are forced to deal with circumstances that are beyond their own control. You can show women who are where you once were that they too can rise above; they too can become strong and make a life for themselves.

She is a woman of strength and dignity, and has no fear of old age. Proverbs 31:25

Day 26

Many women deal with guilt and unhappiness when they go through a divorce but Christ can help restore that happiness and gladness to the heart. You can take this time to use your testimony to show others that they can be happy again, you can find joy and gladness and that it is ok to be happy. When some might say that you should be unhappy, you should be remorseful; Christ says that you should have joy in your heart because you were able to rise above the hurdles that were set in your way. Your testimony to help others rise is only going to give you more hope, more happiness, and more joy. They need to know that joy is not wrong, you can be happy again and that is perfectly alright.

A glad heart makes a cheerful face, but by sorrow of the heart, the spirit is crushed. Proverbs 15:13

Day 27

Your testimony is also your chance to further yourself from those who do not wish to see you succeed. Personal testimony is a tool that can truly help you ferret out what people are supportive of you and what people are not. This is a chance to truly see what you can do and to see what others can see in you. Personal testimony offers a platform for you to show others that you had people who were toxic in your life and that you left them behind.

Make no friendship with a man given to anger, nor go with a wrathful man, lest you learn his ways and entangle yourself in a snare. Proverbs 22:24

Day 28

Your testimony should be tailored to help those who are in need and should not contain any harsh words that would make you seem spiteful, that would hinder your own personal growth as well as the growth of those whom you are helping. Testimony is your chance to show others that even if you do feel angry, you do have regrets, you do not have to act on them, and you do not have to say harsh things to feel better about yourself.

Reckless words pierce like a sword but the tongue of the wise brings healing. Proverbs 12:18

Day 29

Testimony is essentially the fruit of the tree of life in a way. This is what you have gained through the rough times, what you have gained by weathering the storms. This is your chance to do what you can and to really show others that they too can learn and grow. Growth is possible if you take the time to speak kindly and to really try to grow. If you take the time to tell people your story you can truly inspire them to change and inspire yourself to keep changing as well.

The fruit of the righteous is a tree of life, and he who wins souls is wise. Proverbs 11:30

Day 30

Charm can go a long way for good but it can also do harm. Keeping this in mind is one way to tell others that you may be tempted by people who charm you to say horrible things with which you may not be comfortable. In the end it is your own choice and you should keep your own true self even if it is difficult and even if it does not seem like it is going to make a difference.

Charm is deceptive and beauty is fleeting; but a woman who fears the Lord is to be praised.
Proverbs 31:30

A Clarity Tip Regarding Testimony

Testimony is a powerful tool and used correctly it can make a huge difference. With the right inspiration on your end and the right inspiration for those with whom you are sharing your testimony with, you can truly make a difference and help those who are working with you to become the women that they want to be. Your testimony can help to make you a stronger person while empowering others to make a change in their own lives for the better.

You Are Called To Lead

When you are learning your way through your testimony and discovering your calling into leadership, please pray for wise advisors. Their words come from a place of good will and will bless you. Do not assume that all advice is ok. This is where prayer is important in determining what is wise counsel and what isn't.

The lips of the wise give good advice; the heart of a fool has none to give. Proverbs 15:7

Day 1

It's now time to help others to feel their own self-worth. Do not let those you talk with be tempted to feel sorry for themselves. A good motto is, you are strong no matter what anyone says. During these first few days following a divorce help others to take the time to set smaller goals for themselves. One of the most important things you can do as a leader is help others see that they have value.

She is clothed with strength and dignity, and she laughs without fear of the future. Proverbs 31:25

Day 2

Don't sweat the small stuff. As a leader it will be your job to let others know that if you are overwhelmed sit down and take a minute to breathe. Though it may be tempting to do everything that you normally do, now is a time where time management is crucial in your success of helping others. In a leadership role look to help others set small goals and time management so they too can get on the path to recovery.

Above all else, guard your heart, for everything you do flows from it. Proverbs 4:23

Day 3

It is very crucial that as a leader you help others shy away from the temptation to bash their ex or do things they will regret. Often times when we are hurt the first thing we want to do is to inflict the same hurt on others. In many cases, it may seem like the only way to feel good about your self is to make others feel equally bad. Though this may seem like a viable option to them, your task is to shift the focus instead on what that person can do to make themselves better. It is always best to focus any negative energy that they have on things that are positive and that can help them toward recovery.

My sons, if sinners entice you, do not give in to them. Proverbs 1:10

Day 4

Identify your own potential. This is a step that will make any woman a better leader almost instantly. Sit down and think of all your positive attributes, the things that make you strong, what qualifies you to be a leader, and then start to strengthen those traits. It may seem like a long arduous road, but the end result is well worth it. A great place to start is leadership within the bible. There are various stories of leaders in the bible. Take your time and learn what Gods word says for you.

She makes linen garments and sells them, and supplies the merchants with sashes. Proverbs 31:24

Day 5

Draw on the word of the Lord to help you see your
purpose. If you feel that you are not strong enough
to be a leader, turn to God and He will help you
see that you are strong enough and that you do
have what it takes to be a strong leader. If you are
sure of yourself you can help others with no
problem and being a leader often helps lead to
further self-recovery and healing.

The name of the LORD is a strong tower; the
righteous run to it and are safe. Proverbs 18:10

Day 6

Listen to advice from others in leadership, it may help. There are plenty of people in leadership who are worth listening to. It is always helpful to hear from others who have gone down similar paths. If you have a friend or colleague it may be beneficial for you to ask questions about how they began to help others with recovery, and what tips they may have for your own journey.

If you had responded to my rebuke, I would have poured out my heart to you and made my thoughts known to you. Proverbs 1:23

Day 7

Encourage those whom you help to not be afraid to draw strength from scripture. If you have a favorite passage that you draw strength from do not be afraid to let others know where you are getting courage. Encourage them to take their bible with them or to take their favorite passage written on a scrap of paper.

For the LORD gives wisdom, and from his mouth come knowledge and understanding. Proverbs 2:6

Day 8

A strong leader has the ability to forgive their enemies. Take the time for yourself to forgive your ex-spouse and work on helping other women forgive as well. Pray for your ex and teach others to do the same regarding their ex's. Forgiveness is often the first step on the long but ultimately fulfilling journey to peace.

Thus you will walk in the ways of good men and keep to the paths of the righteous. Proverbs 2:20

Day 9

Remember those who stood by you when things got tough. This is why it's important to keep them in your life. Now that you are leading others you will need to draw strength and encouragement from those who stood by you. This will strengthen you and enable you to pour into others and encourage them to find a few friends who are going to stick by them through thick and thin.

Let love and faithfulness never leave you; bind them around your neck, write them on the tablet of your heart. Proverbs 3:3

Day 10

Take time to know that you may not understand,
but God does and he has a plan for you. Though it
may seem like you do not have the power to step
into the role of a leader, you do. God made you
perfectly and he knows that you are strong enough
to be a leader that is why he presents you with the
opportunity to help others. It may seem like
everything is awkward now and that nothing is in
your control, this is where you need to really let
God take the wheel but remember this is a time
when it is more important than anything else
because now others are involved. If you have a
chance to really let go and let God, do it.

Trust in the LORD with all your heart and lean not
on your own understanding; in all your ways
acknowledge him, and he will make your paths
straight. Proverbs 3: 5-6

Day 11

Assure others that their path may not be clear but they can make it. Some days are going to be far harder than others. At times, it may seem like you are not going the right way or that you are not making the progress that you feel you should be. It is crucial that as a leader you are able to tell others that they do have a path that has been cut through stone for them and you are going to help them find it. These are the days when you should lean heavily on God and on the fact that you have a path. It just may not be crystal clear at that exact moment. Let yourself go, let the path be a bit foggy and go forth with the understanding that God loves you and is at your side.

Have no fear of sudden disaster or of the ruin that overtakes the wicked, 26 for the LORD will be your confidence and will keep your foot from being snared. Proverbs 3: 25-26

Day 12

Take each day as it comes, try not to plan too far
ahead. This can apply to both your leadership role
and to everyday life. Though a leader needs to be
organized, there will be things that pop up that you
may not be ready for or that you may not expect.
Take the time to think about how to handle any
situation and be ready for surprises. Though it may
be tempting to plan out each and every day from
here on out so that nothing surprises you, it is far
better to take small steps and set one foot in front
of the other. You will be leading others to do the
same, so it is important that you lead by example.

Commit to the LORD whatever you do, and he
will establish your plans. Proverbs 16:3

Day 13

Teach others to let themselves laugh. Laughter is often the best medicine. There is no real way to start healing if you do not do so with an optimistic heart. The best way to boost your optimism is to realize that there are still wonderful things in the world and you deserve to be happy. Try to find a way to help those whom you lead to find their own happiness again, let them know that laughing is healing.

A cheerful heart is good medicine, but a crushed spirit dries up the bones. Proverbs 17:22

Day 14

Learn; take the time to better yourself. Read about leadership, take advice from others, take the time to really immerse yourself in the role of a leader and it will start to come naturally to you. It is far easier to be a leader when you are equipped with the information that you need to do so.

Wisdom is supreme; therefore get wisdom.
Though it cost all you have, get understanding.
Proverbs 4:7

Day 15

Help others to know that they should not speak ill of those who have wronged them. That sort of negativity will do no one any good. Again, though it may make them feel better for a moment or two to talk down about their ex or to talk about their new partner, it will not help them on their own positive journey. Teach them how it is far more productive to focus on their own strengths and on their own good traits and how they are going to use them to not only rebuild their life but also to become the person they want to be after a divorce. Help others see the potential in themselves and see that positive energy is going to do far more than harsh words.

Put away perversity from your mouth; keep corrupt talk far from your lips. Proverbs 4:24

Day 16

Find ways to let those whom you lead know that it is ok to let their loved ones help them. If they have someone willing to help, let them help. Help does not make you weaker, it only makes you stronger. So help those you work with know that help is going to be needed at some point in their life, no matter how strong they may seem to be.

As iron sharpens iron, so one person sharpens another. Proverbs 27:17

Day 17

Let the Lord into your heart as you start your new journey. God can help you in ways that you can only imagine when it comes to being a leader. He can help give you strength, courage, and a sense of self when it comes to sharing your journey and letting others know that you are there for them in their own time of need. Though it may seem as if you are the only one making decisions, the Lord does work in mysterious ways as they say and he is putting decisions before you to see how you handle them. If you let the Lord into your heart you can begin to see where he is guiding you. Ultimately, God only puts the options in front of you, how you handle them is your own decision and your own path. Though the Lord does have his hand in your own personal journey, you must take the first step if you ever want to get to the final destination that he has planned for you.

In their hearts human beings plan their course, but the LORD establishes their steps. Proverbs 16:9

Day 18

To be a great leader you have to be able to admit that you to need help. Though it may seem like you have everything in order, there is always room for God to help. It is one thing to say that you need help but to really start the healing process you must be able to admit to others the ones whom God has entrusted in you care.

Pride goes before destruction, a haughty spirit before a fall. Proverbs 16:18

Day 19

Lean on positivity and make sure you are positive as much as possible. This will help you see that you are growing as both a leader and as a woman and it will make the journey that much easier and more joyful. Positivity can make a huge difference when it comes to doing something new like leading. Help others to understand that it is far easier to heal if you have a calm and gentle environment and making sure that you use kind words is one way to make sure that everyone is on the same page and everyone is focused on true spiritual and physical healing.

A gentle answer turns away wrath, but a harsh word stirs up anger. Proverbs 15:1

Day 20

Help others learn how to deal with family life and the way that divorce is affecting their children. Often time's women come to leaders for help with their children. Help them understand that a child has no concept of why mommy and daddy are fighting; they do not understand why one parent is not living with them anymore. Help those you lead find ways to talk to their children and really learn how to deal with the debris of divorce.

Those who spare the rod hate their children, but those who love them are careful to discipline them. Proverbs 13:24

Day 21

Let others know how your personal healing is progressing. Sharing your own story is one powerful way to lead. It not only helps you, it also helps those whom you are leading. Sharing personal testimony is just one wonderful way you can learn to be a better leader. In most cases, they will share in your victories which will make them that much more meaningful and will make the journey easier. A support group is a great way to make sure you have people who know your struggle and that want to see you succeed. There are plenty of programs out there that have teachers and leaders that can give you advice and that will cheer you on when you succeed.

A friend loves at all times, and a brother is born for a time of adversity. Proverbs 17:17

Day 22

Determination and steely resolve is the backbone of a leader delivering any assistance in a recovery plan and once you have chosen the path to your own recovery, don't waiver unless you feel comfortable doing so or unless it was your idea to do so. When you know in your heart that God gave you the desire to help someone in need then you do just that, you help.

The highway of the upright avoids evil; those who guard their ways preserve their lives.
Proverbs 16:17

Day 23

Personal understanding is something that everyone wants and that not many people actually achieve. Know that you can gain personal understanding by helping others. When you help others you bless them and yourself because you discover your strengths and weaknesses. You can hone your skills and better develop yourself all while gaining personal understanding and teaching it at the same time.

The beginning of wisdom is this: Get wisdom. Though it cost you all you have, get understanding. Proverbs 4:7

Day 24

Teach others to keep scripture close; this will give them that extra bit of encouragement, when they may need that little boost to keep them going. Also keep your Bible near and keep your favorite passages on hand and actually read them. It may even help to read your Bible daily to draw inspiration from the stories of those who have suffered and overcome with the help of the Lord. If you feel that you are not doing what a leader should do just step aside and let God help. Turn to your Bible to help get inspiration for ways to help those whom you lead.

Get wisdom, get understanding; do not forget my words or turn away from them. Proverbs 4:5

Day 25

Encourage others to not let other people make decisions for them. If they feel like it is a bad idea or they do not want to do it, encourage them to not be pushed for the sake of their friends or people that they know. Make sure they know to stay strong and true to the person they are and want to be.

Charm is deceptive, and beauty is fleeting; but a woman who fears the LORD is to be praised.
Proverbs 31:30

Day 26

Leaders need a bit of time to relax as well. Take time to think about all the things you have done and think about how you will continue growing and leading those who look to you for advice Take a day to really relax and let yourself rest. Also, take this time to pray for your own personal prayer life. Strengthen your foundation during this time in order to continue to build a leadership path that one day others can grow to follow.

In all your ways submit to him, and he will make your paths straight. Proverbs 3:6

Day 27

In leading others, stress the fact that God put you together in this very moment for a reason, he created you both and God loves you both unconditionally. God does not make mistakes and it is more important now than ever for the person to realize this. Each of you has something to give the other. Allow God to use both of you in this healing process.

The LORD brought me forth as the first of his works, before his deeds of old; Proverbs 8:22

Day 28

A leader can do so much but if she has too much on her plate it is not going to help her lead others. Take time to take out the things that are unnecessary and focus on helping others heal and on your own continued healing.

Go to the ant, you sluggard; consider its ways and be wise! Proverbs 6:6

Day 29

Understanding will come to you through God with time. Being obedient to the call on your life to help others is the biggest confirmation that you seek Gods will and HIS will only on your life. God will help you if you call out for help and you continue to keep him in your heart even after you feel you have a good grasp on your role in leadership. It may seem that you have received God's healing through Jesus and you can stop worrying so much, but God can continue to help you grow long after the wounds of divorce have scabbed over.

Indeed, if you call out for insight and cry aloud for understanding. Proverbs 2:3

Day 30

Love yourself and what you have accomplished. You should take time to really appreciate what you have done not only for others but also for yourself. Being a leader is not something that everyone can do. It may seem easy at first but it is far from it. Know that the Lord is also proud of what you have done and He has many great things in store for you in the days and years to come.

Many are the plans in a human heart, but it is the LORD's purpose that prevails. Proverbs 19:21

Meet the Author: Charis Rooks

Divorce is not as cut and dried as everyone imagines it to be. It is a struggle, a challenge, and a true test of character. As not only a survivor but someone that flourished after divorce, Charis Rooks is ready to help inspire women going through the same struggle to rise up. Charis was able to move past her divorce to found Divorce Recovery Advocates Working for Women LLC (Draw for Women) a life after divorce recovery organization that focuses on forward movement and recovery for women after divorce.

As a woman who has been through divorce, Charis knows what it takes to become a strong independent woman despite the scars which divorce leaves. When she is not working to empower her fellow women, Charis spends time with her daughters helping them to become the strong women she knows they are destined to be. She and her daughters currently live in Kentucky where she is pursuing her bachelor's degree in Business Technical Management with a concentration in Small Business Management and Entrepreneurship. Charis leads by example and works to show women that though divorce can hurt a woman, it cannot break her.

This devotional was designed and written with women in mind. The work focuses on helping women work through the stages of grief and healing after divorce to find a personal relationship with themselves and with Christ to heal and work through the process. Charis helps women work through a variety of issues related to divorce and the struggle to regain life after she knows what it is like to feel like there is no hope.

Charis is passionate about speaking the truth and working to spread the word of Christ and its healing power. In addition to Draw for Women, Charis has also: been a speaker, a Life after Divorce Care facilitator and a facilitator for Divorce Care support groups. She is a member of the Professional Women's Network, has taken part in the American Association of Christian Counselors, and the International Christian Coaching Association. Charis has also achieved several certifications including being certified as an International Women's Leadership Coach with a specialization in women's empowerment, confidence building and professionalism. She has also achieved certification with the American Association of Christian Counselors as a life coach with a specialization in life after divorce coaching. Charis is also the author of the Draw4Women, The 30 Day Life after Divorce Prayer Challenge.

Charis is dedicated to her craft and to making sure that every woman who is struggling with divorce knows that there is hope, there is a way to succeed.

Charis is a dedicated individual who wants nothing more than to share her ideas, experiences and knowledge to help other women who are struggling with divorce to become comfortable with themselves and with the state of their lives again.

Contact:

Charis Rooks

Divorce Recovery Advocates Working for Women LLC

http://www.draw4women.com

Email: info@draw4women.com

Facebook: http://facebook.com/draw4women

Twitter: Charis Rooks @draw4women

Instagram: Draw4Women

www.ingramcontent.com/pod-product-compliance
Lightning Source LLC
Chambersburg PA
CBHW072002090426
42740CB00011B/2048